LUCKTOWN

BRYAN PENBERTHY

LUCKTOWN

The National Poetry Review Press
Aptos, California

The National Poetry Review Press
(an imprint of DHP)
Post Office Box 2080, Aptos, California 95001-2080

Printed in the United States of America
Published in 2007 by The National Poetry Review Press
ISBN 978-0-9777182-7-6

Acknowledgment is made to the editors of the following publications in which these poems, sometimes in slightly different versions, first appeared.

ACM: "Lucktown"
Bat City Review: "Goodbyetown" and "Lovetown"
Blackbird: "The End of Free Love" and "Noah Studies"
The Carolina Quarterly: "Electric Alchemy"
Chrysalis: "Bartown" and "Icetown"
Coal City Review: "Thanks" and "Through Ice"
Crazyhorse: "Endtown"
dig: "Crazytown" and "Doubttown"
Ellipsis: "Ocean Songs"
Flint Hills Review: "Take Your Medicine"
Mangrove: "A Toast"
Mantis: "Expatriatetown" and "Hometown"
Möbius: "Oceantown"
New Delta Review: "Dreamtown"
New Orleans Review: "Sleeptown"
Poetry International: "Elegytown"
River Styx: "Bats"
Twilight Ending: "Maledictiontown"
West Branch: "Tigertown"
The William and Mary Review: "Montage"
Willow Springs: "Utah Before Stars"
Wisconsin Review: "Pooltown"

Thanks also to *Mad Poets Review* for reprinting "Oceantown," to *Verse Daily* (www.versedaily.org) for reprinting "Lovetown" and "Sleeptown," to the Association of Writers and Writing Programs (AWP) for selecting "Utah Before Stars" as a 2000 Intro Journals Project Award winner, to Truman State University Press for naming this manuscript a finalist for the T. S. Eliot Prize, to Elixir Press for naming it a semi-finalist for its 2006 Poetry Book Awards, and to the National Federation of State Poetry Societies for naming it an Honorable Mention in the 2006 Stevens Manuscript Competition.

Contents

○ Lucktown

Stay here long and the close calls will turn you into glass.
Half the people in town will die weird: freak storms, tempers,
bad decisions; but always one person staggering
back from the wreck, wide-eyed, to tell what happened. It is
always chance; the bus slides off the road, twenty-three kids
drown, the driver walks away. A hospital snatches
lightning from seven miles out, a hundred burn, but

a candy-striper breaks a window, tosses herself
into the three-story air, lands alive. This one guy,
Mike, famous in town for his escapes, now operates
as an oracle, predicting malady and harm.
By high school, he'd perfected his art of avoiding
girls, close friends, extra-curricular activities.
Above his door, there's a small sign that reads *Survival*

is the worst thing that can happen. His biggest error,
he tells customers, was asking for a pet one year.
That Christmas, his parents bought him a German Shepherd
puppy that he named Sally. A few years later, she
went rabid and bit her way through a screen door, killing
his mother and turning her shivering grin his way
before his father, home early with a headache, shot

into the room and tackled the thing, stabbing at it
with a screwdriver, struggling while it bit and bit
and bit everything flesh. The house stunk death. Only Mike
survived. He says that his craft is easy: look for chance,
for possibility; if found, eliminate it

swiftly. *You can't have luck without disaster,* he says.
Good fortune is merely a condition, but luck is

months of skin grafts, arms that don't grow back, anything close
enough to kill you that doesn't. And then you're just a
story, and everyone's talking about how lucky
you were. Later on, at a crowded bar (they all are),
people drink themselves into arguments over who
among them is the luckiest of all. The police
chief who had half his face taken off by a shotgun

suicide attempt, who's since found Jesus? The store clerk,
Janet, thrown from a crash that killed her husband and kids
because she wasn't belted in? Mrs. Flannigan,
fourth-grade teacher and candle maker, who just found out
that she isn't pregnant, isn't diseased from her rape?
In the restroom, graffiti uncoils on the walls
near the toilets and urinals: Luck Is Just A Glass

Of Wine / You've Pissed Away. Lucky numbers?: 9-1-1.
Luck You. It fills every available surface; luck
as a woman, as a twine-wrapped package, as a stroke
of lightning. Mike doesn't agree with any of them.
Luck is a wide-jawed dog, he says before his clients
walk back into the world: *sometimes scary, and sometimes*
carrying the very thing you wanted her to fetch.

○ Utah Before Stars

how brutally well the universe
works to be beautiful
     —*William Matthews,*
     "In Memory of the Utah Stars"

I

Flaws are, unhappily,

rarely fatal. My father

swore. My mother ruined

jokes. I could never lie

worth a damn. But I'm driving

through Utah, it's getting dark,

and in all likelihood

they've already died.

This is a land Van Gogh

would have hated.

All browns and browns,

and greens collapsed

back on themselves. There is

a finality to the dirt here.

You can drive for miles and see

only a single tree. This is the land

of their final collision. Driving

west, out of Durland, their

arrow shot from a flawed bow,

straightened the line they charted

into the side of a school bus.

And now I'm driving to a hospital

in Utah, to find the end

of that trajectory, just
ahead of the dark.

II

Drawing a figure in the dark
takes practice. Shaping the line,
giving matter form. Above
the cool pressure of our Pinto's
back seat, the stars waited
as I copied them into my notebook,
connecting the dots, shaping
the constellations and all
they implied. My mother's scream
shook me from my seven years of sky;
I saw something large ahead,
filling my head with
light, and my stars and I
collided.

III

The stars are disappearing now,
burnt from the sky
by the glow of a familiar city.
They'll be fine, I insist,
they'll be fine, but I can't
even lie to myself
and I imagine that this
is how it was, how Utah looked
before stars dimly filled
the liquid dark, above the dry

and lonely earth, glowing

just out of reach, moving

closer, closer,

closer.

○ Tigertown

And this, a red tiger biting

her way across town, between cars,

casual, gliding as if she

were invisible—and, really,

everyone pretending not to

see her starlit whiskers, her chrome

fangs, loveliness—bright red fur splashed

unbelievable with color.

All things move around the tiger.

Sometimes she snatches a hotdog

from a curbside vendor, sometimes

a baby from its carriage, as

erratic as this tilt-a-whirl

fall, its wet haze. From time to time

she purrs up against a woman,

blesses her fertile, then moves on.

Yesterday, the town held a vote:

Kill the tiger? Build a statue?

Something else? Wary to avoid

misfortune, we elected her

to our currency, a scarlet

icon on tarnished coins. The bronze

is rotting green against the lip

of blood. The tiger is unmoved.

It doesn't matter. Soon, winter

will drive her into another

town. If there is a way to trick

her, someone there may invent it.

Wait. Someone outside just yelled that

she is crouching on the roof of

the distillery, near the church.

Men are locking doors while I write.

◯ Pooltown

How can't you love a place where everything is steady order

and angle? When steadied, one navigates the tables with ease,

conversations—all which revolve around desire: green felt

for leveled slate, the eight ball for dark corner pockets, and an

elusive waitress named Sarah, our lady of midnight beers

and nachos. Nightly, men wager her origin, where she might

be headed—certain only of her impermanence, blue dust

in fluorescent light. She doesn't know the rules to the games, can't

rack the balls with authority, gives bad advice on cue weight,

where to break, whether every night's new stud will make a trick shot

and take her home. They always make their shots. I don't. She goes home

with nobody, regardless. Slips out when we're concentrating

on mere geometry, lost in computation, figuring

out how to keep the elusive pattern going, keep the balls

dropping, dimly clicking against each other whenever they

touch, whether in play or immediately after falling

into pockets. She is the only unsolvable angle

in all of our lonely mathematics; immune to the smoke-

dulled air, symmetry. I'm not saying this carelessly, either—

here, I have seen men break like scientists colliding atoms

into ivory blur, the resulting static a field of

elementary shots. The problem of Sarah is wearing

everyone down. I have seen steady players trembling when

she clears the counters of glass and cigarette ash. Jokes have turned

malign. The players' discouragement is worse than when scratching

on the eight ball, turning a won game into a chalkboard of

failed solutions. But I'm almost certain I saw her standing

near the jukebox the other day, swaying just a little bit.

○ The End of Free Love

And wasn't the drunkest mania we'd ever caught

       like a bad crush

on merlot: days wrapped in wash-dulled sheets, no matter

       the hundred miles

between our cities, their factories like monuments to folly,

       producing only smoke.

It didn't matter that you wanted us to fight in bed,

       urging ourselves

beyond temporary wounds and into permanence; that I was

       unable to admit

reluctance for the mornings I couldn't raise my left arm

       without wincing,

the memory of your teeth a ring around my clavicle,

       a familiar pattern

surfacing. And weren't our complicities like a remedy

       for love, absolution

from the butcher's work those memories would exact? Our bodies

       weren't built to last.

The elaborate mythologies we'd bury in each other

       wouldn't stay put,

rising as bruises, as ravenous ghosts, as inadequate courtesies.

◯ A Toast

Here's a toast to everything I've done wrong,
everything that got screwed up: telling Vicki
that I didn't love her enough to marry her, leaving
her in Kansas, not picking up the phone the night

her mother died, listening while she sobbed
into my answering machine. Here's a toast to lying
to my creditors, lying to my friends, my parents,
telling them that everything is fine, that I'm perfectly

fine. Here's to all the poems I've fucked up, haven't bothered
writing, waited on too long. And here's to my failed courage
the times I tried out suicide like a garage-sale jacket;
shaking out dust, checking the fit. Here's to nights

I passed out in cars, in bedrooms, hunched over toilets
in fast food restaurants; and here's to all the girls I wanted
to fuck rather than know. Here's to none of it working out.
A toast to knowing I'm in trouble and doing nothing

that could help. Here's to my bad memory, to forgetting
assignments, birthdays, bills, names; here's to my weak
eyes, too quick to cry; here's to my self-pity, my addiction
to being sad, my hatred of both, my pretentious mention

of that fact. And here's to the Ferris wheel endlessly running
these thoughts through my head, that starts up every fall,

the last carnival ride of the season, a mechanical wind

that carries me into winter.

○ Bartown

Choices overwhelm—and here, the regulars

(everyone) argue until you name your

country, your father. They ritualize

the labels from their bottles, will chant mottos

like "Sobriety is the spite of life."

That's your war cry. In dark alcoves, tab men

plot harm for the cash-only crowd, your people.

Tonight, girls—cigarette orchids in smoke-

light—have come to sing evening to a close.

You feel tired. Tribal. Lonely as a mole.

○ Hometown

Too early here and the wind seems justly
bitter, screaming at the sorry, bent trees
and the too slow people crossing the street.
Places like this, the wind forgets its way—
like us, perhaps. With my paper, the man
behind the counter told me that things aren't
right, the way they were. He's bluffing. Outside
the store, cars I'll never own are waiting
for either their owners or for me to
quit looking. The news is all bad, always.

It doesn't matter. Remember: no one
here has a home. At night, everyone sleeps
in the parking lot outside the liquor
store. I rarely sleep. Mostly I just watch
the constellations. Sometimes I start to
build a shelter—usually after
word of yet another possible threat.
Last week it was bad meat; this time around
it's people wearing orange. The rumors
never pan out. Neither do my lean-tos.

There's just not any real danger, unless
you count the town's suspicion industry.
My neighbors accuse me of harboring
criminal dreams. *Give over,* they declare,
we're on to your game. The policemen are
many, and vigorous. Resisting them

is like arguing with graves, or fighting

the spread of sand in that desert to which

the guilty are sent. I might be sent there

soon. I can't believe I live anywhere.

O Expatriatetown

Every building a café, a nightclub,
both, languid beauties tonguing the lips of
cappuccino cups, feeling if it's cool
enough to sip. Every statue is a
writer you've gotten drunk with, a painter
you've laid, carved by a sculptor who respects
you. Everyone here has read all your books—
even the bad ones—and loved every phrase.
Every sandwich you order is perfect—
the Reubens not soggy, the Romaine crisp.

Nights are opiate in their languor—warm,
narcotic. Every woman adores you.
The violinist at every café
plays your favorite songs, sad ones, music
to make your life seem a good decision.
Luckily, bars never run out of wine,
low conversations, and exotic brands
of cigarette. The only province you
can't leave is the country of suspicion.

The papers have it right: celebrity
is the only politics. Happily,
your reputation has grown mildly
comfortable. You are writing a great

novel, an epic about the war years,

which you can't seem to recall in any

great detail anymore—not in this town.

○ Electric Alchemy

This sick November

smolders like a beer

bottle full of fire

flies. Like A.M. radio

dials. Like all the bits

of myself I break

out and throw into

the sky just to spend

all night rearranging.

The world's frequency

is fall. I used to

imagine my eye was

the earth's magnet.

Radio waves

sliding through the air

and into my body,

moving things inside,

electric alchemy

transfiguring the bone

geography into

something harmonious

and resonant, veins

wavering like thin

birch branches, like

dowser's wands.

◯ Ocean Songs

I — Lafayette

It always comes to this: heavy coats, gloves, long johns,
scarves, a flask full of fire, knock-around boots,
a tin harmonica, two biscuits in Nick's coat pocket.

By the river a concrete lip juts above the brown water—
an old access point that now serves little purpose
but as a resting place. We come here cold evenings

when the moon sinks into sky from its secret home
under the currents. The river itself is a dark,
shallow thing—more useful for reflection than fish.

Its surface catches the town's glow, a half-lit stretch
of light pollution wavering, clouded like it was returning
the Milky Way, and not merely human obligation

to negotiable nights. These the mid-winter days of thinking
ourselves the only ones capable of such languid
debauchery, whiskey and sunsets, lights across the water,

an Indiana evening when the world has finally given up
on coming back from its frozen daze, the weather
as schizoid here as anywhere Midwestern; West Nile

mosquitoes hovering yards from the creeks and river

that water the town and keep all waters going, thready fonts
to a somewhere ocean, a life of floating in a less

alcoholic way than this, surrounded by citronella
candles, clear glass bottles, any chemical we need
to perfect ourselves, while we constantly fail.

II — Charleston

The seasonal reluctance to yield to Spanish moss and scotch,
Folly Beach and the asphyxiate jellies, their split atom bodies
coating the shore like empty baggies filled with saltwater.

Sparrows crenellate the sagging power-lines
that grid the air, like smoked glass shattered
and cemented into the crests of fence

that ward thieves past the old neighborhood's
backyards. The midnight sky is full
of algae; the ocean is above us,

it's somehow escaped and we're under
an onyx sea full of stars and water,
a thousand candle-flames alight in current,

perfection amusing as we drift in all our trouble
and happiness. It's okay. Not every boat
is a perfect boat. Sometimes one just floats

atop a plank, with a friend named Jim,

a fishing pole, a corn-pone tale, a love

of adventure.

O Oceantown

Love, the water's skin is an endless bolt

of fabric, a fine-threaded garment of glass

and azure, a mute sheet undulating above

an infinite weight. Tonight the weather is drunken,

shouting at the sand-filled palms and picking fights with gulls,

while all the waves purr to the beach like cats

in heat. But here, I can think only of you,

your lips translating these storm-stained colors, turning

them to tidal melodies that I could even hear

a thousand miles underwater, calling me to port.

○ Lovetown

Maybe the streets go in circles for reasons
you've not deciphered—surely there is some kind of order,
some kind of reason to the erratic map,

the buildings made of glass, translucent bellies
revealing shops filled with crap nobody needs but lovers—
sappy cards, figurines, dead roses that have

already been pressed and dried to save time. Here,
restaurants are crowded with couples pressed together, hands
engaging in their tender ministrations.

It is love, surely, that keeps the leaves turning
perpetually from green to fall's caramelized mauves
and tans. This could be the best place you have known,

except you are conspicuously alone.
It wasn't always this way. Strangers who claim to know you
keep coming up and asking after Sarah,

a name that seems important to figuring
out something key about your isolation, but you have
no news. Your answers leave them unsatisfied

and anxious. It's like carrying terrible news
to Hamlin: the streets clean and gleaming, the children vanished.
There have been studies: a noted psychiatrist,

Dr. Robinson, claims love is merely fear

of being happy once and then losing it forever.

The baker downtown argues love is hunger:

is taking famished bites from some uncommon dish—

salt-crust salmon, raspberry tort—then endlessly trying

to revisit that startling first taste. The news

I trust comes from my physician, Dr. Wiens.

Love, she insists, is allergic response, a miswired

reaction to the chemicals nearness stirs

in our bodies; that love is merely the effect

of losing equilibrium. Love as a withdrawal

symptom. But maybe she is wrong too. This morning

I took a walk along the river's bank, skipping

stones across its languid eddies, trying to figure out

just who the hell this Sarah might be, anyway.

According to the paper's headline, *The Only*

Love That Lasts Is Unrequited Love, but everyone here

scoffed. Me, I'm not so sure. It could explain why I

love anything temporal—the light at sunset

crossing the wall of my small room, changing it from shadow

to gold. It explains the girl on the radio

singing *It's gonna be alright*, and sounding so

certain, though I have heard this song at least seven times this

week. I think the river knows more about love than

any of this town's experts. All day it reflects

the leaf-burdened trees and the heavy clouds, never touching

anything but stone and mud. But it never quits.

☉ Sleeptown

Places like this aren't invented.
        The cold, industrial polish of this city
skews light, and what it reflects

        it returns badly. Splitting the landscape,
an obsidian river carves
        silhouettes of brush and rocks, banks strewn with mica

and quartz shards, pale smoke frozen
        in crystal. A storm-split oak arcs into
bridge-lit water, a coral

        reef suspended in dandelion wine. The trees
and half-illuminated
        buildings seem submerged.

        I know so little
about things that matter. How
        to be a good man. Why rivers are constantly

moving, apparently toward
        ends that mean completion. Whether, drinking
their waters, I would forget

        these twilights—the smell of wet brick and broken pines,
indigo and sapphire-troubled
        skies—or drown. My distracted heart beats codes

I'm unable to translate.

The only ritual I know how to perform

is rubbing the sleep from my eyes.

☾ Montage

I would like to have been in Paris in the Sixties.
I would have been a stone in some infrequented street.

Waiting for someone to pick me up.
Waiting to be skipped over water—

Becoming an errant missive, a Morse epigram.
Becoming an ellipses of cool velocity

before inertia gave and dropped me.
Before I would dive, carving awkward half-circles

as I swung back and forth underwater.
As I did when still nine years old, swinging

above playground sand. Swinging my legs
above me when rising—tucking them on descent.

Until I would give up on my private momentum.
Until I would let the chains go and leap into air.

O Quiettown

First off, the sound of your arrival

will be more than most can take. Downstreet,

the Presbyterian church has been converted

to a winery, the bell-less air

clothed now in yards of coal-dark, soundproof

foam. The large fountain at the center

of town is never running, and no

birds ever cluck or pitch near the desolate bowl.

The movie house is always humming

in its soundless way, back-to-back reels

of silvered, silent films. No flags drape

from swaying poles. Waterlogged earthworms

sprawl haphazardly along damp sidewalks, dying

their slow, wormy deaths. And what will feast

on them? You figure bugs, but wonder.

The fountain, you decide, just may be

a monument to sound, its marble

basin an enormous ear turned skyward, hearing

only rain, until at last the bowl

is buried by water. You'll soon break

the coded language of these silent,

puzzled people, you declare. No one

laughs at you. Rather, they shrink away from the noise

you're sure you're making, hands contorting

into shapes like waving lines, like wings.

☉ Doubttown

suspect this, and the suspect

ways trees turn in wind, shoulder

wind away   suspect the leaves

of conspiracy, they've gone

missing, it's winter   winter's

no excuse   suspect your watch

of running fast, misleading,

making you worry, and then

O Crazytown

I remember going crazy easily.

It just sort of happened—one night I'm sitting

at a stop-sign on Claflin Avenue and

bang—realized the streets could go anywhere.

That trees didn't seem to make sense anymore.

In fact, there was no counting on time, no way

to be sure of the color of skies, of cars;

blues that fade into whites, greens that never fail,

not the way my sense of things did, sitting there.

Towns can't make sense. They're not built to last—at least,

not longer than the first people to build them

could manage to stay sane, having done what was

done. They'd tricked even the light into thinking

space wasn't necessary, replaced it with

buildings, noise—places that make us feel like cats

thrown from some unfathomable height, twisting

over and over, straining to find a way

to land on our feet, as if it were nothing.

○ Bats

Nervous mathematicians—they could be proving

anything up there: that the moon is

a placid moth, unbothered by their awkward

machinations; that the earth is a checkerboard of

sorry, dumb luck; that the grids they plot, their

blind parabolas, are a web, a net, some

kind of snare for trapping wind or

bugs or something else. Some say they've

got their legends too, of bats that could almost break

the sound barrier; that could scratch the dark

like a china plate. There could even

be stories about one that gave up the flight-driven life

of snatching iridescent jewels from air,

surrendered his love of charting

the spaces between the small bodies

darting across the sky's dim facade, and became human,

never again slept all day, learned colors. *His life is less*

restless now they squeak, then dive.

◯ Smoketown

Some far-away fire in the night

keeps the blurring moon from breaking

through its hazy shroud, lit orange

by the streetlights and parking lot

halogens and the bit of flame

licking the horizon, wholly

surrounding this town. Some wonder

whether the fire's moving closer

every day, or if it's headed

farther away. Most seem to think

it's not moving at all, is just

burning some buried source of fuel

that has no end. It's possible

to find a way to breathe without

too much effort; mostly people

just get tired of the problems

seeing anything, some nimbus

strain of smoke concealing almost

everything. There's been some minor

talk of sending out a party

to find out what makes the world burn.

There's been this kind of talk before.

Mostly everyone just stays in,

ignoring the smoke as much as

they can, which is an awful lot.

○ Dreamtown

My sister tells me that we must pick weeds from

the dirt floor of the tool shack, while warning me

of a snake, six feet long and quick. I see it

suddenly, the serpent's coiled lunge, and cut

its head half off with a corn knife. Then I peel

the skin back, which comes away wrong; not a slick

roll, but like crust, pieces of particleboard,

and ask my sister whether she cooks the meat.

Only by mistake, she says. I walk back to

the snake's head, which has become a little dog,

almost a breed of dachshund. I start feeding the meat

to it. It skitters around. I name it "Lorena,"

and soon it's coming when called. It is much bigger now.

Distrustful of its slatted eyes, I look for the door

to the shack, but find only rusted tricycles, dried

wasps nests, teeth. The snake-dog edges closer, unhinging

its grinning jaw, consuming wet pieces of itself.

It keeps getting bigger. There's no way to leave the shed.

○ Maledictiontown

The name they give you is foreign.

The milk's gone two weeks bad. All food

is repulsive to your palate,

all but lamb. You are vegetarian.

Keys you need disappear. Pets you love die.

Paint is peeling. Apartments you live in

burn to the ground. Another girlfriend leaves

town, contracts something serious, loses

touch. Every dream you have is

terrifying. Every time

you turn to your lover and try

to say *love* it sounds like *loathe.* When

answering accusations you indict

yourself. Guilt is all you know. Photographs

of you are always misplaced or ruined.

No one calls you up except the police.

Your lungs are always hurting. Your stomach.

Your sister died in a car wreck

three weeks ago, and you only

heard about it this afternoon.

◯ Take Your Medicine

After he wrote the poem he folded the paper into a little square and swallowed it. When he went to work, he kept hoping that someone would notice a change in him, but nobody said anything. Weeks went by. He wondered if the poem was working. Nothing felt any different than before. He decided that he must just be a bad poet, and gave up writing. As an experiment he chewed up a page of Yeats, and felt light-headed. He was sure he was onto a cure. Moving through the library surreptitiously, he cut pages from books with a razor blade for later consumption. By this point he knew people must be pretending not to notice. One day he was eating Randall Jarrell and sliced his tongue, a paper cut in a place he wasn't prepared for. He spent all day in bed. Bowel movements were wracking. He stopped seeing books as anything but flavors now, which in combinations could do secret things inside him. He became voracious. His mouth was a nest of infection, of cuts that wouldn't heal. While eating, he had to pinch his leg to force the pages down. He was sure that he was getting better.

○ Sicktown

Call it what you will—a failure of spirit, of weather,

the sidewalks buried in unswept leaves and bodies

in the streets, crumpled in front yards, the clouded, olive sky

refusing to either sleet or clear to a less ominous sign.

Of course it's screwed up, sitting on this porch, nodding

at the other coughers sprawled in plastic lawn chairs,

all of us watching for who'll drop next or what might come.

Better than the dank air in our boarded-up houses, waiting out

the malady that has beset this town. The world's become

the rattle in my lungs, a cluttered patch of trees

freezing up in December, cottonwood branches cracking

against each other. A film reel of community theater

highlights would have lasted as the best memento

of this final season, until two actors stole

the orchestral brass and woodwinds, then set out to compose

a funeral march to eulogize the town's retroviral end.

It's not bad, really—the tuneless trumpet stutters and spalls,

lacquer flaking trails into the overgrowing

lawn, and the security guard who blows it shuffles out

a third-time jig, his sickness conjectured as rumor from his grin

and stamping boot, his daughter said to be away
from harm in a far-off port city, marrying.
The accordion man, an ex-chainsaw salesman, smothers
his coughs with a bicep, refusing to interrupt his playing.

It may in fact be the end of everything they would love
about ruthless winds and meteorology.
There is no cure for their joy. Say the wrong moon is hanging
in decline—they're practicing lyrics about never buying bread

in the promised land, hallelujah, where our lungs
will be healed through song. They bang their good silverware
against grease-stained skillets, shatter vases through crescendos,
composing their loud catastrophe as an offering to dust

like the only emissaries from a land of no rain.
They aren't getting better. The solo clarinet
is still a step behind the beat, lagging at the edges
of the final, invulnerable happiness in our last days.

○ Assassintown

Little snipers, they—
picking off herons, the sleepy
cormorants, as if they could shoot
to the hearts of impenetrable meanings.
The sky is brittle glass. They say explanations are
unnecessary, that faith is harder than the quartz
which stipples the coastline. Better is the feel
of trigger, rain's coppered scent, smoke
that fills the spaces where they've crouched,
the minutes they've killed.

I wish *I* could pull the trigger.
Here, wind erases granite, transforms
earth into abstraction—everything
becomes abstraction—until
one of the assassins lines up another
animal in his sights and pulls it into
being. We're only as real
as the landscape that shifts around us,
mud flashing pale with either gunfire
or moonlight, ceasing to matter.

They say that all real violence is
unexpected. I won't believe those rumors
again—not after this town, all these rifles
marking the distance from breath
to dirt, soul to flesh. How easily one could collapse
for good in this place, where all that the dead remember

is the final swallowed breath

before the report, and understand why God

embraces sleep, and naps his way apart from

another, better kind of heaven.

◯ Icetown

Blink and the light shifts on you inside the curves
and bulges, pale blues and rippled luminescence, your crystal
everything—but articulation slips

in the optical trick and words lose purchase.
Incandescence spills from chamber to chamber unchecked, dimly
lighting the thousands of erratic cracks

which web the world—as if something were beyond
this antiseptic ice, beyond the fractures of its ever-
changing core, so an exit could be found,

something could be done—but it's settled inside
a much larger sheath of organ and meat, and beyond that words,
and beyond that the nothing that made it.

○ Through Ice

After a photograph of the last passenger pigeon, frozen
in preparation for shipping to the Smithsonian Institution.

I've seen you buried

in the pages of a book I'd forgotten.

How your eyes retreat

into the shadow of your face.

How you've somehow slipped away.

I could look in all the towns,

call your name for hours

and still you'd elude me.

Wrapped in a taffeta of crystal

and mystery, still

after these many years.

The words I want

are wasted ones.

At midnights like these

hope is a thing of fever.

You are gray and gone.

Were you here,

I'd warm your little feet,

wipe the dust from your shoulders.

Wrap you in clean feathers

and send you into the paper sky

of history, the way we do

with all things we've loved

and lost, the way

we always will.

⦿ Noah Studies

rain:

Noah is almost happy waiting for rain. He knows that he'll be happy when it finally starts, as it'll be the only way to prove he isn't mad; he also knows that when it starts everyone dies and so guilt masters him. Noah knows too that during the rain he will be both expecting it to stop anytime and go on forever, wanted and cursed, an unsafe circuit.

birds:

Birds flew by at dusk and Noah's up nine hours, can't sleep with nervous wondering about whether he has two of them already; they were the size of several he'd caged, but the markings, dark arrows buried in feather, looked different; the colors—iridescent, ultramarine—seemed unusual. From the earth he was too distant to make out their species—desert sparrows? Byzantine grackles? And he wonders about the armies of spiders marching into the hold now, hundreds and hundreds of species, thousands of legs scrabbling against wood.

noise:

Raining fourteen days and the noise is enough that he communicates only in gesture with his family, the same way he motions to the confused cattle that mill in their holds, waking from dreams of riverbed and thistle; to the rhinoceri, the bullfrogs, the mambas; to the gorillas, dark hummocks shot with silver, glowering; to the giraffes and koalas and cicadas; to the varieties of hornet and wasp and yellowjacket and bee nest spackling one treacherous, humming wall; the language of the adrift stunning the wood to infinite echo in Noah's head, enduring God's endless bounty.

choice:

Jug of wine and time thinking about choices: eat the goat cheese, the scent of which troubles the coyotes, or thin the potato hoard? Round up the ants, who've escaped their pen and are carting away the grain? Re-pitch the cracked cypress shelves and braces in the lower hold? Burn for heat the sketches he'd tried of the stranger animals, beyond his crude art to depict? He drinks his wine and watches the junk littering the water sink and questions come like heavy rain-drops, like cats batting at fluttering moths, like a chorus of disconcerted angels praising the mystery of doubt.

dove:

What's it like when the dove returns, olive leaf caught in its beak?

Panic.

○ Maptown

Coming down from their demands on weather, conspiratorial,
the cartographers stretch a line taut and pace off distance. The map's not ready.
Three weeks in and still I'm sketching anything but geography,

the rest of the team pacing a weed-snarled outcropping, swearing in
mathematics, some kids dragging the body of a deer through the sycamores,
ramshackle tobacco sheds burnished with October. We've been tasked

with mapping the region, finding a way to permanently fix
this location on paper for all time to come, or however long it lasts.
I pencil in some bramble at the margins of a paper sack,

torn in half and with the shoreline's curve in drafts, as if the landscape
didn't want to be pinned down, was reluctant for overfamiliarity.
We're not the only crew, of course. Pretty much everyone handles

some of the inkwork, except the managers. There is a widespread
rumor that the grids aren't matching up, that the creek in one map
is a river in another. The community's split on reasons. I wondered

for awhile, and then didn't. We can't come to terms on equations
for angle and perspective, while the Indian summer seems the midpoint of
another autumn's long-enamored coma. My version of fall

is written in topographical swirls and the clutter between
their ebbs and affections, the map unfolding like a girl's last sweetheart letter,
her hyacinth throat thick with mourning. Each day loses its color

to the water, scattering to innumerable bright flashes,

every one unrecorded. We follow trails of breadcrumbs and memoranda

back into town, while the pine trees are doing whatever pines do.

O Depressiontown

Being sad is playing fetch
with a dog, throwing a stick into a pond
and watching him paddle out to retrieve it.

For the dog, nothing in the world exists but
completing the circuit, finding what's been thrown
and returning it to you.
After awhile the stick sinks or splinters.
The game ends when there's nothing left to retrieve.

My brand of despair is irresistible.
It operates on me like a vain surgeon,
like fall operates on leaves.

◯ Endtown

Everyone's staring
at everyone else
all of the time. It's
made me a midnight
blue sky crowded with
brilliant junk, it makes
me weep like Jesus.

Einstein was tortured
calculating the world's operation,
figuring out how
the celestial static is—somehow—
non-coincidentally related.
He puzzled over
how in time's dust-veiled basement all things bend
to greater forces than themselves, how all
things end—even stars—
yet the water above is mirrored in
the water below.

These days, I maintain
my own counsel. The
night fires are wide
and lonely; they keep
the dark away for
a time; they curl to
embers, tiny stars.

○ Belle Isle

Let's forget about politics for now, Nicholas, we'll let them lie.
A dog lunges into the James River after a tennis ball and fights
the current as best it can to regain the shore. It doesn't mind
the Union dead, the coming hurricane. It cares only for solidity
and a satisfied hand on its doggy head. I grow angrier at the man
who keeps flinging the ball into the water and refusing to watch
what happens. I keep worrying about the dog.

The ten thousand imprisoned here don't matter anymore, the dead
can't be accurately counted, their ends were miserable and useless.
People will always die. They are unfailing in this, their best devotion.
Here, the river's muscled current and historical placards
are only temporary traumas, none of which matter to the dog.
Nor to us, today. Instead, I'm enjoying the sun in a merciless place,
you and Allegra, this momentary reprieve.

For Nicholas, in the Museum of the Confederacy

Your wife's a blur of red and bone, a smeared photograph.

      She's dead, you're dead, I'm dead.

We're alive, meandering this small mausoleum, finding Stonewall's blood,

the sword Armistead waved past Pickett's Charge,

      his last urge besting any of our pictures, our mawkish stories, outlasting

the dead and their deprivations,

their diaries swollen with earth, their words illegible. Time, old friend,

      is a measure of distance. The camphored sky spills

dusk into the gaps between our cities, spreads a sepia patina over

the year's raw wound, heals into knowable scars.

      The legend's right: we're dust. The medical room's orchestral ghost

plays rusted knives, suffering gone

to cobweb, boxes of metal and gauze, a document for every wounded cry.

      My cry is wounded. My cry's a snarl

of twig and gray fabric, it's a thrush caught in crossfire, minie-balls hissing tunes

from which there's no returning, no math

      resolving. If we won't wake from the coming ether, these words

will have to stand. After all,

consider these props and reliquaries: here's Lee's tent, sparse, here's us,

      a silver flask. Here's Pickett, twenty minutes

before his division's murder, in command and ornery. Here's a brick apartment wall, cracks filled with plastic animals,

      plaster covered in shadowboxes; here's to what little time remains.

If there are legends worth making,

make this one ours: that fevered want and words can drive the dark

      to its amnesiac home. Beyond

the batteries that would saw us down and ruin every town that mattered.

○ Elegytown

Sundays when the miners come to church
to pray away the mountain's weight collapsing,
ward against the shallow, thready air,
the town clenches shut, hard as a fist of lead.

Other days are mirrors made of lead,
all the same: the trudge to the pit's dark swallow;
air snatched, precious as the ore they cut;
the coughing, crushing ache the work pulls from them.

Then the days when the earth closes over them,
collapse being common, braces cracking
deep in the wood. The years when many die,
roomfuls lost to fault and structural failure.

But when they gather to mourn failure, silence
serves for eulogies. Prayers choke off,
black with dirt and stone, that every day might be
the same at the mine: climb in, climb out.

Someday the veins will seize up, mined out; refilled
with iron rails, scrap bins, bitter words;
the air completely stilled, the way it is on
Sundays when the miners come to church.

◯ Hugotown

Last lights dim in windows across streets, end
the try of another day for meaning.
Places are just places—nowhere matters,
the man who earlier cut my hair said
when I asked after landmarks, good eating.

Sundays the townspeople turn out church
socials, parades, recurring garage sales
where they'll buy back the same things they just sold
for more than they made. High-school cheerleaders
chant taunts at the elderly, painful men.

Possibility is the trout's quick flash
of color; a magician's trick, then gone.
There is always another election,
another lake to fish, another way
to hate the thing in you that quits. To walk

past the rows of houses and lit-up bars
is a ghost-dance, a circuit connecting
their roughed-up lives with my own. If I were
to call my ex-girlfriend from here, the words
would strangle in the static of broken

payphones. The people here aren't right. Always
looking for a fight, a drink, ways to hurt
the people they blame for ruining them.
Teens take hundreds of pictures: friends, themselves—

relics—before they are beaten out of

adolescence. However, tentative
breezes kick up most afternoons around here,
relieving the day's temper, rehearsing
the evening's cool whisper. *Honey*, a man
names the river in a tender season.

Later, he mails letters to past lovers,
insisting that his brand of despair is
a mark of character, is endearing.
They're rarely returned. Those that do come back
aren't nearly the kinds of words he'd hoped for.

I'm still getting sidetracked. I wish I knew
what drew me to places like this, people
I can tell stories about, true or not.
That man over by the bank, he might know.
He has a blue balloon, and looks happy.

○ Thanks

Thank you for the moon tonight. Thanks
for the gasoline holding out. Thanks for
no crows on the lawn. Thank you again,

       three times over for that book being right

       where I needed it. I don't need to say

which one—I mean, you put it there. Thank you for
inventing silly language. Oh, thanks also
for the leftovers I'd forgotten. I'm giving thanks

       for fields of wheat gone autumn, brittle

       as frozen lakes, ice in January. Promises

flown too early south for the season. But thanks
for the excuses. And before I forget, thank you
for the caterpillar on the railing. Thank you for

       wind. For bark. For branches that break.

       For clouded night skies, but not so much so

that stars can't get through. Thanks once more
for the thunder with no rain. And thank you
for the blanket you left behind. Thanks.

O Goodbyetown

And this could even be a film: something

is ending, or has just ended. Maybe

a carnival or circus—the rocky

beachfront that faces town is covered in

waterlogged tents, dark blue fabric sinking

in the middle where the rain has gathered.

The ground is torn with massive ruts, proving

a recent history of large machines

that must have moved enormous things into

place. But now there's only stone and water;

a heavy wind that slaps the tents, snapping

sounds from them; this endless, humid August

a violent weather can't quite shake. Last

night I met a girl. I didn't expect

the magic trick she pulled, half-sung lyrics

like mercury, *the moon is a light bulb*

breaking, the derelict sea slipping back

from the rocks to the bay; her hand finding

mine in the dark. Stars crowded the sky, best

friends to any traveler lacking map

or compass. I wanted to navigate

the curved line of her neck with my lips. Cure

the distracted wind of its constant need

for leaving. Fend off the morning and our

inevitable, separate journeys

to other towns. *All things end,* she told me.

Even stars. But I said that I love stars

for their loneliness: unapproachable,

unquenchable, unable to receive

comfort until they burn out whatever

interior fuel that kept their fires

going and become just another hole

in space. She laughed and won me from my bluff.

Stars don't get lonely. For them, all of this

is just a lost-time incident, a kind

of celestial dream before they wake

and remember gravity. All night, we

watched people stagger out of their houses

carrying boxes and lamps, setting up

card tables, preparing for what looked like

another round of yard sales. Yesterday

I walked from house to house, lifting trinkets

from tables as if weighing them, judging

whether they were worth the prices. Never

finding anything I really wanted,

I walked away from tables of clothing

and pans, worn-out books, a broken TV,

seventeen ham radios, piles of

homemade greeting cards. Almost bought one that

was a picture of an open hand, palm

pressed against glass. On the inside it said

Hands are how we touch. Without yours around

I can't feel anything but empty space.

When I went to pay I found nothing in

my pockets except a crumpled Greyhound

ticket to another town, the final

destination indecipherable.

Leaving is what I keep returning to,

how we couldn't keep the dark from slipping

into day, how there was no telling what

distances we'd measure without meeting

again. But there's another part of me

that bets against travel's amnesia,

calculating time against accident.

This morning I woke up early to catch

my bus out of town, but found out that they

weren't running until later in the day.

I guess they figure we need time to think

about the places to which we're headed,

or what's happened wherever we've been. All

the shops I've passed are closed. It seems that most

are going out of business—the many

signs I've seen in windows say everything

must go. I keep going around this block,

eyeing the ocean's calm, watching ships as

they pull away from worn piers. People wave

from the deck at the beach, wave to the tents,

wave at the space they moved through earlier—

floating past the reach of tether, headed

at the line that cuts sea away from sky.

About the Author

Born in Dearborn, Michigan in 1976, Bryan Penberthy currently lives in Charleston, South Carolina. In 2000, while an undergraduate at Kansas State University, Penberthy was selected as an Associated Writing Programs Intro Journals Project award winner for the poem "Utah Before Stars." Its appearance in *Willow Springs* the following winter marked his first major publication.

In 2003 Penberthy completed his MFA at Purdue University, where he received the Leonard Neufeldt Award for his work. During his time at Purdue, Penberthy served as Poetry Editor for *Sycamore Review*.

Penberthy's poetry has appeared in *ACM*, *Bat City Review*, *Blackbird*, *Coal City Review*, *Crazyhorse*, *New Orleans Review*, *Poetry International*, *River Styx*, *Verse Daily*, *West Branch*, and elsewhere.

www.ingramcontent.com/pod-product-compliance
Lightning Source LLC
Chambersburg PA
CBHW022030090426
42739CB00006BA/368